LOVE POEMS

LOVE POEMS

Quentin T. Decker

Xulon Press

Xulon Press
2301 Lucien Way #415
Maitland, FL 32751
407.339.4217
www.xulonpress.com

Printed in the United States of America.

ISBN-13: 978-1-5456-6988-4

TABLE OF CONTENTS

For the Love of Pets and Birds

For the Love of Limericks

INTRODUCTION

In the seventies, there was a very popular song entitled, "The Second Time around." I was married at the time to my first wife, and had no reason to believe that the song would ever apply to me or my wife. But in 1977, we were divorced because of "irreconcilable differences." Suddenly I was in the dating world. What does a 47-year-old father of three know about dating? I had been married for 20 years, and now I'm not.

After moping around the house for a while, I finally got the courage to ask Betty, who was a co-worker and a friend I had known for 9 years. She was a single mom with four kids, some of whom were students of mine. We dated for two years, and during that time, I was inspired to write poems to Betty almost every day. I used to put them in her coffee cup in the lounge.

We finally decided that we should put our families together and get married—we were crazy about each other. Pages 1 – 8 are a few of the better ones. We traveled a bit, and I was really inspired after visiting Civil War battlefields.

For The Love of God, pp. 9 – 17, will show just how much God has become a part of my life, especially since Betty and I have been married. She brought me back to Jesus. Pg. 15 is dedicated to the survivors of the recent fires, floods, and earthquakes. Although they may have lost everything, they are still thanking God for another day.

Pp. 18 through 23 are fairly self-evident. I hope you will be pleased with what you are about to read and that you can relate to some of the feelings we all may have experienced at one time or another.

Enjoy.
Quentin T. Decker

ACKNOWLEDGEMENTS

Thank you, Mom, for showing me the difference between right and wrong, raising me as a church goer, and waiting at the pier for Dad to come home from the sea.

Thank you, former students and fellow teachers who encouraged me to publish.

Thank you, Betty Lou, for loving me, understanding me, and inspiring me to write poems about love.

Falling in Love

FIRST DATE

by Quentin T. Decker

A tall woman in a white dress
Standing in the driveway.
A gracious lady holding my fingertips at dinner.
Or taking my arm as we cross the street.
A gentle listener to my problems
Who offers advice and help.
A sweet friend who gives me her full attention.

We danced the night away,
I knew the guys in the band.
They loved her right away.
Should I ask for her hand?
No! On the first date? Get real!

February, 1978

Presence

by Quentin T. Decker

All that I see here
Is All that I need:
Your sweet presence.

There Is a balm

You are like a balm
With which I cover
My anxious self, the lover
You spread your goodness over me
In soothing, smoothing ecstasy.
You take away my loneliness.
You heal me with your pleasantness.
I get "balmed" on you!

Prancer

Do you have a prancy walk
That really turns me on?
Whenever you walk through the room,
I cannot stare too long.

WHO KNOWS?

by Quentin T. Decker

Tender, girlish face,
Our romance is so new,
How are we to know
If love is really true?

Smiling, Irish eyes,
Our time is all too brief.
Far be it from me
To cause you any grief.

Sweet consistency,
My wounds are with me yet.
Healing will take time.
Some things I can't forget.

Loving, feeling lass
Whose feelings never fail,
Don't you know at times
Our logic must prevail.

Honest lover mine
If I seem distant now,
It's only a slow speed
My logic will allow.

Burning passion fire,
You've taught me how to love.
Maybe you were sent
To me from God above.

SWEET

by Quentin T. Decker

Got to bed this morning;
Didn't make a peep.
Couldn't tell for sure
If I was smiling in my sleep
—probably was.

Chocolate covered cherries sweet
Will tell you how I feel
Sometimes I have to pinch myself
To see if you are real
—probably are.

YOU LET ME BE

by Quentin T. Decker

Getting to know you is interesting.
You make it very easy because
You're so easy to be with.
I can be myself, and you like that.
When I can be myself around you,
Then I get to know myself.
Because you let me be me,
Getting to know you is getting to know me.
Ya' know?

CLOUD NINE

by Quentin T. Decker

What have you done to me?
You know how I hate heights.
But I'll be okay
'cause I know you're up here
...' with me.

BREAKTIME

A face smiling in the window,
A visitor at my classroom door.
I open it and hug the trim, warmly-dressed form
That smells of fresh night air and outdoors.
I kiss the smile on her face. . . .Hi, friend!

MY PRAYER
ON A BEAUTIFUL DAY

2-16-1978

by Quentin T. Decker

Great God, as I look up and all around me, and I see
Your marvelous works, Your awesome power, and
Your infinite beauty, I am reminded of my own small
self and that I am just a tiny speck in Your grand
scheme of things. Yet, I do not feel insignificant
because I know that You saved me for a purpose,
that I am your child, and You listen to your children
when they speak to You.

I pray today that You will guide me in everything that
I do—in every decision that I make. Teach me to be
compassionate and loving of others, help me to know
what is right in my relations with others, especially in
affairs of the heart, with which I seem to be so preoccupied
lately. Help me understand my emotions
and not let too much logic stand in the way of them.
On the other hand, grant that I may not be overcome
by my emotions so that sound reasoning is crowded
out. Help me to say goodbye to the past, to forgive
myself, as well as others, and forget. I look forward
with happiness to each day that You make and of which
You allow me to be a part.

Amen.

For The Love of God

GOD'S LOVE

by Quentin Decker

God's love is like Chaucer's April rain.
It pierces my drought-ridden March soul
with such sweet showers
that my sins are forever washed away
And virtue is again reborn.
Like the little green buds on the vines,
I have truly been given another chance
to become a beautiful person.
I cannot live without God's love
Anymore than a flower could exist without the rain.

CONSIDER THE LEAVES

By Quentin Decker

How gracious is the "fruitless" mulberry
That stands so tall inside my garden gate.
How fitting is its lesson there for me,
That I begin to wonder and to wait.

And soon the miracle that one perceives:
The barren stubs in spring give birth to arms.
By summer, arms are hidden with new leaves.
That glisten green and shade me from sun's harms.

In Autumn, yellow takes the place of green;
And, changing thus, the leaves dispute it not.
For, gracefully, these leaves have always seen
That turning brown and falling is their lot.

They do not hasten their demise one hour.
By living fast and ripping life away.
The only drug they need is that sweet shower
That comes upon a wet and rainy day.

As gold turns brown almost before my eyes,
I watch the magic leaves begin to fall.
And, full of hope, I come to realize
That "fruitless" doesn't fit my tree at all.

I've learned a simple lesson from my tree.
As gently now I prune the yearling wood.
If I can, aging, just as graceful be,
I'll know my path is leading where it should.

Then will my time as patiently be spent,
As mulb'ry leaves, their single season gone.
They showed the truth to me before they went,
And bore much fruit for me to think upon.

ANTIETAM

by Quentin T. Decker

How came I here? I cry
without a sound
What is this carnage lying all around?
These bloody, broken bodies at my side,
What stroke of fate is it I haven't died?

I push bodies off me with a groan,
And clutch my chest as heavy as stone.
Ah, yes, it seems, if mem'ry
serves me well,
I led the Charge, and suddenly I fell.

"Jake" bucked me off, I must have
hit my head.
They've gone away and left me
here for dead!
Dead thousands choked the field
wherein we ran,
And Jake would never step upon a man.

What hell has come upon us
here today?
The twisted, headless boys in
blue and gray
Who line the sunken road, the
bloody lane,
Oh, God, I pray they did not
die in vain.

I struggle to my feet and look around.
Where tall corn grew there's only
smoking ground.
I stagger up the hill the church to find,
Where waiting friends perhaps my
wounds will bind.

When suddenly among the
smoke and soot,

A hand is clutching firmly at my boot.
I hesitate and gaze upon a face
Of fear and rage, of pain and
youth—a trace.

"Kill me, Yankee!," whispering he begs.
I stare at dirt below where were his legs.
"Kill me, sir," he notices my sword.
And I cannot pronounce one,
single word.

"I love you, brother," finally I say.
"Though I wear blue and you the
rebel gray.
And kill you was my mission
'ere we came;
But, if I kill you now, I'll take
God's blame."

"Kill me, sir, it's such an easy task.
If you love me, you'll kill me as I ask,
And I see God today, I'll say that you
Were all I ever loved that wore the blue."

I draw my blade that idles at my thighs
But, as I raise it up, my comrade dies.
Then I fall, weeping, on it's golden hilt.
The sword I never used brings
only guilt.

What hell has come upon us
here today?
The twisted, headless boys in
blue and gray,
Who line the sunken road, the
bloody lane.
Oh, God, I pray they did not
die in vain.

WAITING AT THE PIER

by Quentin T. Decker

My sweetie is coming home today,
At least, that's what I heard him say.
After all that he has seen and done,
Will I still be his number one?

Can I turn his heart around,
And shut out all the other sound?
Will he look the same as when
He promised to come back again?

And do I look okay today?
(This wind has blown my hair astray.)
I'm wearing his favorite color—green.
And holding the daughter he's
never seen.

"Oh, look!" yells someone in the din.
"Oh, look! The ship is coming in!
And soon the band will start to play
As anxious spouses crowd the quay.

The gangway touches starboard side,
And then my tears I cannot hide.
Four wounded, bandaged
patients smile
Their gurneys guided down the aisle.

As many couples now embrace,
My eyes are searching empty space.
When, suddenly, up near the bow,
I think that I can see him now.

"Sam!" I scream, and he sees me
And waves his hat most franticly.
"Brenda!" he yells out very loud,
Then pushes his way through
the crowd.

We don't quite know just what to say
But hugs and kisses have their way.
"God is good," I want to pray,
Waiting at the pier today.

THEY HAD TO LEARN

by Quentin T. Decker

It was sad, you see
To be a Saducee
And not fair, I see,
Who was a pharisee.

Because they
couldn't see
And they couldn't hear
And they didn't know
That God was near.

They questioned Him,
He put them down
"You bunch of snakes,"
Would cause a frown.

"This man is bad.
He's got to go.
(He's bad for business,
Don't you know?)

"Let's pay His friend."
He heard their thought.
Unknown to them,
He knew their plot.

And on the Cross,
He paid the price
For all our sins
And all their vice.

It was sad, you see,
To be a Saducee
The day He rose
For you and me.

And, in their turn,
They had to learn
That this pariah
Was their Messiah.

by Quentin T. Decker on November 4, 2017

GOLGOTHA

by Quentin T. Decker

Between two thieves, they hung Almighty King
And, for all our sins, He took the blame.
His followers weren't there to see the thing
That frightened hearts would only bring them shame.

Lord, You've done no crime that I can see.
I know we thieves deserve this for our vice.
When You come into Your House, remember me.
And He said, "You'll be with Me in Paradise."

The soldiers did not know what they had done
When they nailed Him to the Cross: God's only Son.
Then Jesus asked His Father to forgive;
Took their sin upon Himself, so they could live.

They placed a crown of thorns upon His head;
And, mixed with precious tears, our Master bled.
The day grew dark; the ground began to shake.
They pierced Him, though His limbs they did not break.

Near the end, the human Son was crying out,
"Eli, Eli, lama sabach thani?"
And what that meant to those who heard Him shout,
Was, "God, oh why have You forsaken Me?"

The Holy Temple's veil was a rent asunder.
God's love for His Good Son was not diminished.
And even through the quake and crashing thunder,
Jesus' final words were: "It is finished!"

THANK YOU, GOD, FOR ANOTHER DAY

Thank You, God, for another day.
Guide my footsteps along the way.
You've come into my heart to stay,
And I want to live for You.

Thank You, God for another day.
Keep me faithful so I won't stray.
You have washed all my sins away
And given me life anew.

(bridge) "Let the words of my mouth and the thoughts
Of my heart be acceptable in Your sight, Oh,
Lord, my strength and my Redeemer."

Thank You, God, for another day.
At Your feet my heart I lay.
You're the truth, the life, the way.
I'll follow you all life through.

Floods, and fires, and shaking ground,
War and terror and sin abound.
On my Rock, I'll be safe sound,
As long as I trust and obey.
Thank You, God, for another day.

WE HUNG OUT

2 Peter 1: 13-18

Peter wants to remind us all,
Before he answers The Father's call,
That he and his friends hung out with the Lord,
Who spoke the truth like a two-edged sword.

They did not invent these marvelous things.
"Cunningly-devised fables" they did not follow,
But were eye-witnesses to the King of Kings.
Anything else would have been so hollow.

They heard this voice which flowed like a fountain,
When they were with Him on the Holy Mountain,
Saying, "This is My Son in whom I am well pleased."
Then they fell on their faces; with fear they were seized.

They watched in amazement (as Jesus designed):
Lepers' flesh healed; sight to the blind;
A crooked body made straight and good.
Maybe God did this! Who else could?

by Quentin T. Decker
A.r.r. 9/12/2018

MY JESUS

If you offered me the world,
Without my Jesus,
I would have to turn you down
And say, "Goodbye."

For I always will reside,
With Jesus by my side,
In a house that riches could not buy.

He was knocking at the door I finally opened.
Since He came into my heart, I'm born anew.

When I'm going to face the trials
Than come along the miles,
My Jesus will be there to help me through.

Bridge:

My Jesus is your Jesus
He loves everyone of us the same.
Our Jesus is their Jesus.
Every knee shall bow and praise His name.

For The Love of Children

NOW YOU KNOW

As you gaze thoughtfully at your little gift from God,

And you sense the helplessness and dependency in those trusting eyes,

And you pray God to make you equal to the task before you,

The bonding begins: The anxious smile of recognition for only you,

The wild glee of play that only you elicit,

The desperate tears that only you can soothe.

It is then and only then that you begin to love in a way you've never known.

It is then and only then that you begin to understand

Your own parents' constant hovering

When you were looking up,

And holding on

To the giant fingers.

Golden days

To adore a Deodora,
Is appreciation highly.
To climb a Deodora,
Is another thing entirely.

Little wooden stepping bars
Some 2 x 4's would do,
And Danny Decker, fearlessly,
Climbed up to see the view.

"Enjoy it, son," said hopeful dad,
"And surely mind your grip."
So Danny held the branches firm
As cross-trees on a ship.

And so this piece of rugged mast
Suffices to remind us:
A sailing ship in our front yard
And the Golden Days behind us.

..........with all my love,
Dad

For the Love of Pets and Birds

KIT

He clung to life tenaciously.
Just as he had to win the tug-o-war.
But, always a gentleman, he let go of the rope.
Just at the right time.
God was pulling on the other end.

Was there ever a friend so true?
Was there ever a dog so cute?
He could get a smile
From even the most stern-faced folks.
"Oh, look, a Corgi," they would say.
And stoop to meet his loving eyes.
And pet his warm, tri-colored coat.

Good night, dear Pupper, and we will miss.
Your sweetness and charm; but we know this:
You're in Heaven, and you're so glad.
To be chasing a ball for Mom and Dad!

Q. Decker 9/21/2010
2:30 a.m.

Beau

The island in my kitchen
Is the domain of Beau,
The kitty with the appetite
Like none you'll ever know.
He crouches near the "crunchies"
Making sounds one would abhor
If that doesn't get my notice,
He knocks them on the floor.
If I try to walk away,
He reaches with his claw
As if to say, "C'mere old dude.
I need to fill my maw."
And so I really must give in
To this cat's funny habit.
It's costing me a lot of bucks
I should have bought a rabbit.
But first, because they've made a deal,
Grandma comes and hugs him.
He rolls his eyes as if to say
That this stuff really bugs him.
"Get on with it! " He softly purrs.
"Open that can and feed me!
If Beau could open it himself,
I'm sure he wouldn't need me.

Q. Decker

Sandpipers' Dance

Waiting for the wave to slide up the shore,
The brave sandpipers chase it back down.
And, as quickly, poke their beaks in the sand
They seem to know when to fly and to land
They poke and they dance all around, you see,
In hopes of catching a delicious sand flea.
They are not deterred by an occasional gull
Nor do they mind waiting for the quiet lull.
If you love birds and the seashore's romance,
Then come and watch the sandpipers dance.

SNICKERS

Snickie, wickie, Snickie boy
You're my little Corgi joy.
Soft and tan with little white paws,
Your smile brought so many "aaws."
You've gone to Heaven after 13 years,
We said goodbye today with tears.
And yet, we know you're in God's care
Because He welcomes Corgis there.

7/4/2018

For the Love of Limericks

1
LIMERICKS

Driving a car without brakes,
I shouldn't.

If I were in my right mind, I wouldn't.

The Brake Shop said, "Why?" And
here's my reply:

I tried to stop by, but I couldn't.

2

A wise old man from Japan
Said this about alcohol ban:
A man takes a drink,
The drink takes a drink,
Then, finally, the drink takes
The man!

Writing a limerick is easy
My ideas just come in so breezy.
I try to be clever
And think, "Oh, whatever,"
But sometimes it just comes off

CHEESY!

3
LIMERICKS

By Q. D.

Everyone drives too fast
At 70, I usually get passed
By a guy who is racing
Or a cop who is chasing
No, thanks, I would rather be last.

So I have decided, you see,
That the freeways are just not for me.
Well, I'll stick to the side roads
And a few of the wide roads,
A safer way and just as free.

What will they think of next?
Does everyone have to text?
If I have my choice,
I will hear my wife's voice;
A phone call is what she expects!

5/28/2017

4

I find it abundantly clear,
When I think of a billionaire:
If he would just park it
In a one percent market,
He'd earn $10,000,000 a year! (do the math)

Thank God for the lovely rain.
It's so nice to have it again.
We're sick of the drought
That has put us all out
And the heat that affected our brain!

5

Sir Henry Morgan was knighted
In spite of the towns he blighted.
It caused me to wonder
How such a huge blunder
Was never royally righted.

With due respect to technology
I feel that I owe an apology
When we talk about "apps,"
I want to take naps,
Respecting the more my biology.

About the Author

Quentin is a native of San Diego, California. He completed his studies in Business Education at San Diego State University and began teaching high school courses in Gregg Shorthand. After earning a Master's degree, he "moonlighted" at a local community college teaching Business Communication. He played Sax or piano in a jazz combo on weekends. After retiring from teaching, he became a model and a movie extra.

His love of poetry began in the ninth grade Print Shop class. He set type, inked the press, and ran off several copies of "The Psalm of Life" by Henry Wadsworth Longfellow. He loved it and memorized it. College courses in poetry helped him to learn about rhythm and style.

He and his wife, Betty, live in La Mesa, California. They are both active Christians. Fortunately, all seven of their children are living successful lives in the San Diego area.

CPSIA information can be obtained
at www.ICGtesting.com
Printed in the USA
BVHW011741091219
566081BV00017B/1666/P